Flowering
House Plants

MINEKE KURPERSHOEK - PHOTOGRAPHS: NICO VERMEULEN

 **REBO**
PRODUCTIONS

©1997 Rebo Productions, the Netherlands
© 1997 Published by Rebo Productions Ltd.
text: Mineke Kurpershoek
cover design: Ton Wienbelt, The Hague, the Netherlands
picture editing: Marieke Uiterwijk
editing: Elke Doelman, TextCase, the Netherlands
layout: Signia, Winschoten, the Netherlands
typesetting: Hof&Land Typografie, Maarssen, the Netherlands
translation: Euro Business Translations, Bilthoven, the Netherlands

editing, production and overall coordination:
TextCase Boekproducties, the Netherlands

ISBN 1901 094 642

Contents

Foreword

Many years ago, as a Dutch student living in England, I read an article in an English newspaper asserting that the Dutch were so poor that they often couldn't afford curtains, so they put lots of plants in the window to stop people from peering in. My landlady in those days used to bring her friends upstairs to see this strange Dutch girl's room, full of plants. How times have changed! While the Dutch have lost none of their love of house plants, the British have become increasingly captivated and now also surround themselves all year round with beautiful plants, many of which originate from tropical and subtropical regions. As well as a huge range of foliage plants with every conceivable leaf shape, colour and pattern, there is a tremendous selection of flowering house plants. This book deals solely with the flowering house plants that bring colour to our living rooms and windowsills.

Since not everyone knows which plants will flourish on a windowsill that gets the sun all day, or on one facing north, where there is light but no sun, the first chapters of the book look at what different plants want in the way of position. This means that you can make a list of suitable candidates before you set off to buy plants for your windowsill. Obviously you don't have to stick strictly to the species listed for each window – for one thing, your house probably doesn't lie exactly north-south or east-west – but you will in any event have an idea of what the plant needs. The amount of water you should give a plant is equally hard to specify, but if you know enough not to keep a water plant in desert conditions or stand a desert plant in a saucer of water you will at least be heading in the right direction.

Of course there will always be people with green fingers who can successfully grow a shade-loving plant on a south-facing windowsill, but they really are the exception.

The last three chapters are devoted to different groups of plants – trailing and climbing plants, bulbs, tubers and rhizomes, and some of the orchids and bromeliads.

Lastly, I would like to take this opportunity of thanking Peter Wolters, who works at the famous flower auction centre in Aalsmeer, Holland. With the range of plants available growing almost by the month, I turned to him for advice. He has been of immense help, and was also kind enough to correct errors in my text relating to the care of the various plants.

Mineke Kurpershoek

Pelargoniums and fuchsias in the Royal Conservatories in Laken, Holland

Introduction

If you have a wide windowsill, it will be easier to create an attractive grouping in your window than if the windowsill is narrow. On a narrow windowsill you will be forced to stand your plants in a row. Try putting a group of the same plants next to one another, or place them together in a long, narrow trough or basket. A wide windowsill offers more scope, and you can create a good basis of foliage plants with contrasting heights, leaf shape and leaf colour. This forms a superb background for your flowering plants. Be sparing in the use of plants with variegated leaves, because the flowering plants will not show up well against them and the whole effect will be confused and messy.

The same thing applies to your choice of cache pots or containers for your plants. Too many different cache pots in all the colours of the rain-

Flowering plants in the Royal Conservatories in Laken, Holland

bow and with all sorts of decorations distract attention from the flowering plants and produce a busy and fussy effect. If you are particularly fond of decorated pots, limit the number you use and intersperse them with plain pots in a toning shade. This creates a more harmonious effect and also shows the decorated pot off to best advantage. A window full of plants looks much more effective if you use containers made from a single material. If you have opted for baskets, don't put decorated pots in among them; instead partner your wicker and willow baskets with wooden boxes. Zinc has recently come back into fashion, and as well as the usual buckets and bowls, you can now also find other zinc items that you can add purely for decoration such as a watering can and a pitcher. Terracotta is very attractive too, but when buying do make sure that the pots are glazed inside. If they are not, you will have to stand them in a glazed terracotta saucer. Another option is to make the pot itself watertight. There are terracotta saucers that are said to be watertight, but which do in fact let water through after a while. Either don't buy this type, or replace them.

Plants that live on a windowsill above a radiator often have a very hard time of it in the winter. The rising hot air flows over the leaves and shoots that protrude beyond the windowsill, which can cause them to dry out. When the curtains are drawn in the evening it creates an insulated zone between the window and the curtain, inside which the temperature can fall dramatically. If the window is well insulated or double-glazed this is obviously far less of a problem than when cold air can get in through gaps and cracks. Flowering plants with soft leaves are particularly susceptible to the effects of the hot air from the central heating and the cold nights. Try

Right: the simple addition of a pottery frog brings an extra dimension to this group of plants

to make your windowsill as wide as possible so that plants are less exposed to the heat rising from the radiator, mist regularly, preferably in the morning, and keep the humidity up by standing the plants on wide trays containing pebbles with water in the base. In very cold weather, with severe frost, you can move the plants to a slightly warmer spot at night.

In a garden centre your eye will often be caught by a particularly lovely flowering plant that you simply can't resist. You bring this magnificent specimen home and display it in all its glory on your windowsill, but after a few days it starts to look decidedly less happy. You will wonder why. It may of course be to do with the amount of water you are giving the plant, but there is a very good chance that it is simply in the wrong place. Light – too much sun, too dark – is one of the most crucial factors in the health of your plants. This is why, in the next three chapters, I have grouped the plants according to the position of the windowsill to which they are best suited. You shouldn't treat this as a hard and fast rule; some plants can sometimes stand on a south-facing windowsill, provided they are given pro-

A basket of begonias

tection if the sun is full on them all day. Similarly, shade-lovers on a north-facing windowsill can tolerate a certain amount of sun, so they could be given a position facing east or west.

Left: foliage plants form an attractive background for flowering plants

Below: baskets of all shapes and sizes

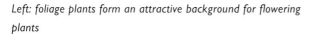

A south-facing windowsill

A south-facing window usually presents problems, since there are very few plants that can take exposure to full sun all day long, let alone cope with the high temperatures. Many of these plants can tolerate more sun outside, because fresh air is circulating there. As you read the descriptions of these plants, make a note as to whether they will need some protection from the sun and keep your eye on the humidity in hot weather.

A beautiful pelargonium

Beloperone (shrimp plant)

ORIGIN: Mexico

The decorative value of *Beloperone guttata* comes not from the flowers, but from the green shading to pink bracts, which overlap to form a long, shrimp-like spike. The small, white tubular flowers drop quickly, but the bracts remain on the plant for months on end. The shrimp plant can grow into a substantial shrub. Every part of this plant is covered with downy hair.

CARE

The plant needs a lot of water during the growing season, and should be fed weekly with a fertilizer for flowering house plants. Do not over-mist plants with downy leaves since the moisture evaporates slowly at cooler temperatures and this can lead to rot. Protect the plant from the sun during the hottest part of the day.

The Royal Conservatories in Laken, Holland

Beloperone guttata

In winter put the shrimp plant in a cool place (about 15°C, 60°F) and cut down on the water, but never allow the compost to dry out completely. Repot in spring and prune as necessary. This plant will not tolerate the smoke from cigarettes and cigars or the ethylene gas given off by ripening fruit.

Catharanthus (Madagascar periwinkle)

ORIGIN: Madagascar

This sturdy little plant has been grown as an annual for some years now. The leaf has striking veins that are slightly lighter. The single flowers, which may be white or various shades of pink, sometimes with a darker 'eye', are about 3 cm (just over 1 inch) across.

CARE

Catharanthus roseus prefers a sunny position but does not like to be too hot, which makes it a good plant for a container outside. Keep the compost moist at all times and feed once a week. Leave the plant to overwinter at about 15°C (60°F). Cut it back in spring and pot it on. Use the shoots you take off as cuttings, which will root readily in water.

Chamaelaucium

ORIGIN: Western Australia

Although this is a new arrival as a house plant, it has been familiar as a cut flower – or, more accurately, flowering branch – for several years now. Little clusters of tiny white or pink flowers develop between the needle-like leaves, and will remain on the plant for a very long time.

CARE

This is really a patio or terrace plant, which means that *Chamaelaucium uncinatum* prefers to spend the summer outside and should over-winter in a cool place (a few degrees above freezing). Keep the compost moist at all times in the summer and let it get fairly dry in the winter. Feed with a house plant fertiliser once every two weeks.

Euphorbia (crown of thorns)

ORIGIN: Madagascar

In the euphorbia family, it is the bracts rather than the flowers that provide the colour. The stems of the varieties and cultivars of the compact *Euphorbia x keysii* and *Euphorbia milii* are sticky. The bracts vary in colour from white through yellow to red, and there is a range of

Chamaelaucium uncinatum

Catharanthus roseus

Euphorbia milii

Euphorbia milii *'Pyramid Eyes'*

pink shades. The common name warns you that the branched stems are covered with large, vicious spines.

CARE

During the summer, when the plant is in flower, the compost should be kept slightly moist. Overwatering or underwatering will result in leaf drop. Use tepid water for this plant, and feed it every two weeks. The crown of thorns will not tolerate cold or draughts. The plant can be kept cooler during the dormant period in the winter, but the temperature should not drop below 15°C (60°F). Cut down on watering and do not feed the plant. Repot it in a mixture of two parts loam to one part soil.

Eustoma (prairie gentian)

ORIGIN: the southern part of North America and the West Indies

The well-known cut flower *Eustoma grandiflora* (syn. *Lisianthus russellianus*) has recently appeared on the scene as a flowering house plant. Growers keep this biennial small with the aid of growth inhibitors. The magnificent large, poppy-like flowers in white, pink, blue or purple show up well against the waxy grey-green foliage.

There is also a white cultivar with a purple edge. The leaves are placed in pairs on very slender stems. The flowers grow from the leaf axils either singly or in clusters.

CARE

This plant, which is a native of very dry, sunny regions, loves the sun and needs very little water. Add some house plant fertilizer to the water (at room temperature) once every two weeks. There is no point trying to keep this plant once it has finished flowering.

Gerbera

ORIGIN: South Africa

This familiar cut flower can also be bought as a pot plant. The foliage and flowers are not unlike those of the dandelion, but larger. The daisy-like single or double flowers are carried on long stems. Gerberas are available in a wide range of colours and shades, with the exception of blue and purple. The small-flowered, short-stemmed varieties make the best house plants.

CARE

Shield this plant from too much sun. The compost should always be moderately moist, but must never be too wet. Add house plant fertilizer to the water once every two weeks. Gerberas will also grow outdoors in the summer. You can overwinter them (at 15°C, 60°F), but they will not flower anything like as well the following year.

Eustoma grandiflorum

Gerbera

Gerbera

Hibiscus (rose of China)

ORIGIN: Southeast Asia

The single trumpet flowers of the Hibiscus are perfectly set off by the glossy, dark green leaves. There are double-flowered varieties and some with streaked petals, too, but the single varieties are by far the most beautiful, mainly because the long, overdeveloped pistil with its striking stamens shows up so much better. The blooms come in a range of colours, with the exception of blue or purple. There are also cultivars with a variegated or crinkly leaf, but they tend to look as though there is something wrong with them.

CARE

Outdoors, *Hibiscus rosa-sinensis* can stand full sun, but on the windowsill it will have to be protected from the sun during the hottest part of the day. Keep the compost moist during the growing season and feed with house plant fertilizer once every two weeks. Mist regularly with softened water. You can leave the plant in the living room throughout the winter, or put it somewhere cooler – in which case you should cut down on watering and stop feeding it. After a few years, once the growth inhibitors used to keep it compact have lost their effect, the Hibiscus will grow into a sizable bush. If necessary, cut it back in spring.

Keep the plant in the same position relative to the light source, otherwise it may drop its flower buds. Cold and insufficient humidity can also cause bud drop. Avoid draughts, which can encourage aphids.

Hibiscus rosa-sinensis

Hibiscus rosa-sinensis

The hibiscus can go outside in the summer

Below: Nerium oleander

Kalanchoe

ORIGIN: Madagascar

There are a great many Kalanchoes, and they are quite different from one another. *Kalanchoe blossfeldiana,* or flaming Katy, is an old favourite with fleshy, glossy, dark green leaves and clusters of tiny flowers in white, cream, yellow, orange, pink, lilac or red. Short day treatment by the growers means that flowering plants are on sale all year round. The miniatures are simply ordinary plants that have been treated with a growth inhibitor. Crosses with the creeping *K. manginii* and others have resulted in some very attractive cultivars with elegant, pendent bell-shaped flowers. The most popular are 'Mariko', which has small flowers, and the larger-flowered 'Dream Bells', 'Tessa' and 'Wendy'. These are often sold in hanging pots.

CARE

The fleshy leaves are an indication that the plant can tolerate quite a lot of sun, although it should be moved temporarily or given some protection if the sun is scorching hot. Take care not to over-water. To encourage flowering, keep the plant cool over the winter (10-15°C, 50-60°F), water sparingly and do not feed it. Make sure, too, that the plant does not get more than ten hours of light a day. Repot in spring in compost to which you have added some clay and sand, and prune at this time if necessary. Once the danger of frost has passed, the hybrids of *K. blossfeldiana* can go outside in a sunny spot, where they will flower profusely. Since they are succulents they will require little in the way of water. Do not dead head them, since new blooms keep developing on the top of the old flowers.

Nerium (oleander)

ORIGIN: Mediterranean

The oleander is a shrub that grows all around the Mediterranean both wild and in cultivated form. People often bring a cutting of this plant back from a Mediterranean holiday. The lance-shaped, leathery leaf tells you that the plant can tolerate a great deal of sun. The white, cream, salmon, pink, soft red or lilac flowers are borne in clusters at the ends of the stems and adorn the plant throughout the summer. There are also semi-double varieties and varieties with variegated leaves.

Kalanchoe 'Wendy'

Following pages: Kalanchoe blossfeldiana

Below: Kalanchoe 'Tessa'

CARE
To keep your plant healthy it is best to put it outside for the summer. Give it plenty of water during the summer, feed it once every two weeks, and mist regularly with lime-free water. In winter, put your *Nerium oleander* in a light, cool place (5-10°C, 40-50°F). Water very sparingly and do not feed. Keep out of draughts or you may encourage scale insects. Prune after flowering to prevent the plant from getting leggy. Leave the young shoots, because this is where the new flowers are forming. Propagate in summer by means of semi-ripe cuttings, which you should pull carefully from the plant. Root the cuttings in water or moist compost. Every part of this plant is poisonous.

Pachystachys (lollipop plant)
ORIGIN: tropical South America
There are two varieties available in the shops – *Pachystachys lutea*, which has yellow bracts and small white flowers, and *P. coccinea*, with green bracts and red flowers. The bracts overlap to create vertical spikes.
CARE
These plants need quite a lot of water in the summer and the occasional feed with house plant fertilizer. Bear in mind that they like very high humidity.
They should overwinter at a temperature between 10°C (50°F) and 15°C (60°F). Prune the plants during this dormant period, and then bring them back into growth in spring. Like many other plants, *Pachystachys* is treated with growth inhibitors and will grow into a large plant once the effect wears off.

Pelargonium
ORIGIN: South Africa
Plants in the *Pelargonium* Grandiflorum group, often inaccurately referred to as geraniums, have attractive, light green, slightly rough foliage and fairly large flowers. They are white, pink, red or lilac and often have beautiful markings in the centre.

Pachystachys coccinea

They will flower all summer long on the windowsill, but will also thrive outside. Attractive hybrids have become available in recent years, some of which have much smaller flowers and leaves. The dark red 'Lord Bute' (which I have

Pachystachys lutea

Below: Pelargonium Grandiflorum hybrid 'Velvet Duet'

Pelargonium *Grandiflorum hybrid 'Lord Bute'*

Pelargoniums as container plants

Below: Pelargonium *Grandiflorum hybrid 'Kalandria'*

also seen on sale under the names 'Black Knight' and 'Black Night') is truly magnificent. 'Velvet Duet' is purple with a lighter edge. 'Tip Top' is pink with a dark red spot and the small-flowered 'Kalandra' comes in the same shades, but its spot is less pronounced.

The other flowering pelargoniums, including the ivy-leaved types *P. peltatum* and the zonal pelargonium hybrids, really do better in the garden although the dwarf zonals, among them 'Stadt Bern' and 'Black Vesuvius', can be grown as house plants.

CARE

Pelargoniums have fairly soft leaves, which means they have to be given protection from really hot sun or placed on an east- or west-facing windowsill. Most pelargoniums originally come from the tropics, so they must not be over-watered.

Add some house plant fertilizer to the water once every two weeks. Outside plants must be brought in before the first frost and overwintered in a cool place (10-12°C, 50-55°F). Give them very little water or stop watering them altogether. In spring, plant them or repot them in fresh potting compost, cut them back as necessary and gradually increase the water. This is also the time to move them to a warmer spot. Pelargoniums are easy to propagate from cuttings in the summer.

Rosa (miniature rose)

ORIGIN: various hybrids

This miniature rose for the living room is available in white, yellow, apricot, various shades of pink, and red. They usually have double flowers (although there are some semi-double varieties) with blooms measuring around 2 cm (1 inch) across. Growers are currently conducting trials of large-flowered roses for the house: the Parade cultivars.

CARE

The lighter and cooler the position you give these roses, the longer they will last. Keep the compost moist at all times, use water at room temperature, and mist regularly if the plants are in a warm spot. Feed them with house plant fer-

Rosa x hybrida

tilizer once every two weeks. Always remove the dead heads. After flowering, move the plant to a light, cool place or put it outside in the sun. Keep it frost-free over the winter.

In spring repot the plant in fresh potting compost with added fertilizer (you may want to use special rose fer-tilizer), and prune it. Start giving it more water, and feed again when it comes back into growth.

Suitable climbing and trailing plants

These climbing and trailing plants can be used in a south-facing window:

Bougainvillea

Glory Lily *(Gloriosa)*

Morning Glory *(Ipomoea)*

Jasmine *(Jasminum officinale)*

Passion Flower *(Passiflora)*

Black-Eyed Susan *(Thunbergia)*

Suitable bulbs, corms and rhizomes

These bulbs and corms will do well in a south-facing position:

Autumn crocus *(Colchicum)*
Amaryllis *(Hippeastrum)*
some types of *Oxalis*

Passiflora caerulea

Bougainvillea glabra *'Sanderiana'*

Right: Jasminum officinale

Below: Salmon pink bougainvillea

A windowsill facing east or west

If a window faces due east or west, the sun will only be on it for a short time each day. The sun is still quite weak in the morning, but by the end of the day, when it is in the west, the temperature will have risen and it will be hotter. There are a great many plants that like a lot of light but limited sun. The plants discussed in this chapter like some sun, but not too much, and will consequently be very happy on a windowsill facing east or west.

Gardenia jasminoides

Abutilon striatum 'Thomsonii'

Abutilon

ORIGIN: Central and South America

The white, yellow, orange or red weeping, lantern-shaped flowers of the different hybrids hang decoratively among the pale green 3 to 5-lobed leaves. The foliage is generally plain green, but *Abutilon striatum* 'Thompsonii' has a variegated leaf. This spotting is caused by the mosaic virus, which does not harm the plant. If you want to propagate this one, you will have to take cuttings or you will not get the spotting in the offspring. Abutilon can grow into very tall, shrubby plants, so older specimens are best suited to a greenhouse or conservatory.

CARE

If the abutilon is in a warm place, it will require a lot of water and a weekly feed. The plant will appreciate a spell outside in the summer, in light shade. Do not expose the variegated-leaf types to the sun. Overwinter the plant at 10-15°C (50-60°F) and water very little during this period.

Cut back in spring and repot in ordinary potting compost with the addition of dried farmyard manure. The plant is prone to attack by red spider mite, whitefly, aphids and scale insect if it is placed in a draught.

Right: Aphelandra squarrosa

Below: Abutilon *x* hybridus

Aphelandra (zebra plant)

ORIGIN: the tropical rain forests of Central and South America

Aphelandra squarrosa is a plant with very striking foliage – green with bold cream leaf veins – from which it derives its common name. Spikes of overlapping yellow bracts rise jauntily above the foliage.

Tiny yellow flowers form between the bracts, but rapidly drop.

CARE

This is a fairly demanding plant to care for. Use softened water at room temperature, always keep the compost moderately moist and mist regularly, because it likes high humidity. Feed with a house plant fertilizer once a week. Overwinter in a cool place at 10-15°C (50-60°F) and water very little during this period.

Aphelandra prefers a window facing east or north.

Begonia

ORIGIN: tropical and subtropical regions in Asia, Africa and America

More than a thousand species of begonias have been described and there are also a great many cultivars. Most of them are foliage plants which have beautifully marked leaves and produce attractive flowers too.

There are also begonias that are grown specifically for their flowers, such as the *Begonia* Elatior Group, with double flowers that look like little roses, and the single-flowered hybrids of *B. lorraine.*

The Elatior hybrids, which are available in a wide range of colours, are on sale in shops and garden centres all year round. The white and pink *B. lorraine* hybrids flower in autumn and winter.

CARE

Most begonias have fleshy stems and foliage – a

Begonia *Elatior Group*

Begonia

Begonia *Elatior Group*

clear indication that they cannot tolerate strong sun. However, they do need a lot of light. Never let the compost dry out, but take care not to overwater since this is fatal.

Avoid draughts, which can make the plant prone to mildew. The best way to water begonias is to stand them in a saucer of water or pour water into the cache pot. Check after an hour, and tip away any water that is still left. Once a plant has been attacked by mildew it is generally past saving.

Give begonias a weekly feed with a house plant fertilizer while they are in flower. Try to avoid temperatures above 20°C (70°F).

Browallia (bush violet)

ORIGIN: South America

Browallia speciosa is an attractive shrubby perennial with white-throated blue flowers. It is usually grown as an annual. The plant will bloom profusely for an extended period if you pick off the flowers as they fade.

CARE

Do not allow the compost to dry out, and feed the plant weekly. It prefers a cool spot. You can raise the bush violet from seed or propagate it from cuttings. There is no point in keeping the plant once it has finished flowering.

Begonia *Lorraine Group*

Brunfelsia

Brunfelsia

ORIGIN: Central and South America

When it is flowering this is a magnificent plant, but not everyone will succeed in keeping it in bloom. The almost round, violet-blue flowers are borne in clusters. After a few years *Brunfelsia pauciflora* var. *calycina* forms a spreading shrub with beautiful, glossy foliage.

CARE

This plant likes plenty of light but cannot take full sun. It can go outside in the summer, when the fresh air will do it good. If possible, use soft water for watering and keep the compost moderately moist the whole time. Feed once every two weeks. You can encourage bud formation by putting the plant in a cool place for the winter (12-15°C, 55-60°F), reducing the amount of water and feeding only once or twice.

Campanula (star of Bethlehem)

ORIGIN: Northern Italy

The star of Bethlehem, an old-fashioned house plant, is a member of the campanula genus that we know as garden plants. *Campanula isophylla* 'Mayi' has blue flowers, while 'Alba' has white ones. The trailing stems make this an ideal hanging plant.

CARE

The campanula only forms buds as the days get longer – it is what is known as a 'long day' plant. Growers artificially extend the length of the day

Left: Browallia speciosa

for these plants so that they can have flowering plants available for sale all year round. The star of Bethlehem likes plenty of light but will not be happy with too much sun. Water freely in the summer and feed with house plant fertilizer once a week. Overwinter the plant somewhere cool (5-10°C, 40-50°F). Cut it back in spring and repot it in a light potting compost. Never leave water standing in the pot since this will cause root rot.

Chrysanthemum

ORIGIN: China and Japan

Botanists have recently decided that the *Chrysanthemum* should be known as the *Dendranthema*, but the new name does not seem to have caught on. Chrysanthemums are excellent as cut flowers, but they are also much-loved garden and pot plants. The pot chrysanthemums (the

Campanula isophylla 'Mayi'

Campanula isophylla 'Alba'

Chrysanthemum Indicum group) are ordinary garden varieties that have been treated with growth inhibitors to produce a compact, bushy plant. The chrysanthemum blooms in the autumn, but even this is manipulated. By cutting down on the light in summer or providing extra light in winter, growers are able to supply flowering plants at any time of the year. Chrysanthemums are available in a huge range of colours – the only exception is blue.

CARE

Keep your chrysanthemum as cool as possible and out of the sun. Make sure that the compost is reasonably moist at all times and feed the plant once every two weeks. Once it has finished flowering you can plant it out in the garden, but do bear in mind that it will grow taller than it did as a pot plant.

Curcuma (turmeric)

ORIGIN: India to Australia

This is an exotic plant with very unusual flowers. It is actually the attractively coloured bracts that make the plant so ornamental. They shelter tiny white or yellow flowers that are virtually invisible. *Curcuma zedoaria* is available as a cut flower and a house plant. The shoots of the plant are edible. The roots are used as a flavouring and in medicines.

The ground roots of *C. longa* are a traditional component of curry powder, giving it its yellow colour. Turmeric is also used as a yellow pigment for dyeing fabric. *Curcuma* is a member of the ginger family.

CARE

These plants need a lot of heat and high humidity. They do well in a window facing east or north, because they like plenty of light but no sun. Keep the compost moderately moist and feed occasionally with a liquid plant food. The leaves will turn yellow as winter approaches, and this is the time to put the plant in a cooler place (10-15°C, 50-60°F). Give the plant just a little water from time to time. Repot it in early spring, dividing the root if necessary. Gradually move the plant into the warm, and increase the water once the tips of the first shoots start to show.

Cytisus (genista)

ORIGIN: Canary Islands

Cytisus x *racemosus* is an attractive shrub with fine, grey, downy foliage and small, fragrant yellow flowers borne in long sprays at the ends of the shoots. You will find genista in the shops in early spring.

Chrysanthemum *Indicum Group*

Curcuma zedoaria

CARE

Do not put this plant in a warm, dry room or it will rapidly drop its leaves and flowers. Keep the compost moist and feed the plant with house plant fertilizer once every two weeks while it is in flower. When it has finished flowering, cut the shoots that have borne flowers back, and put the plant in a slightly shady spot in the garden. Bring it back indoors in the autumn and keep it in a cool place (5-10°C, 40-50°F) during the winter. Move it to a warmer spot in early spring and gradually increase the amount of water.

Erica (Cape heath, Christmas heather)

ORIGIN: South Africa

The cultivars of *Erica gracilis* with their white, pink and pale purple flowers are sold in the autumn. The woody, compact little shrub is covered all over with needle-like leaves and masses

of bell-shaped flowers. *Erica* x *willmorei,* which has spikes of long, tubular flowers, is particularly attractive. This plant blooms in April and May.
CARE
E. gracilis will soon drop its leaves and flowers in a warm living room with low humidity so you should put the plant in a very cool place, for example in an unheated porch, or water and spray it frequently with softened water. There is no point in trying to keep the plant once it has finished flowering. *E.* x *willmorei* also likes a cool position. Cut it back lightly after flowering, put it in the garden and bring it back indoors in the autumn for a second flush of flowers the following spring.

Euphorbia (poinsettia)

ORIGIN: Mexico, tropical South America
Euphorbia pulcherrima, a plant sold in its millions around Christmas time, bears insignificant flowers and striking bracts, which can be white, pink, salmon, red or bi-coloured. In its native regions, the poinsettia will grow into a substantial bushy shrub. You can buy it as a dwarf or tall bushy plant, or as a miniature (it will have been treated with growth inhibitors); they are even occasionally grown as standards.
CARE
The poinsettia likes plenty of light and in winter, when the sun's rays are fairly weak, it will even tolerate quite a lot of sun. Keep the compost moist at all times. It is really not worth the bother of trying to keep this plant once it has finished flowering.

Erica gracilis

Exacum (Persian violet)

ORIGIN: The island of Socotra in the Indian Ocean
A compact little plant with glossy green leaves and a profusion of tiny, almost round violet or white flowers with a striking little tuft of yellow stamens in the centre. Miniature versions are available; these have been treated with growth inhibitors.
CARE
Exacum affine is grown as an annual and there is no point trying to keep the plant once it has finished flowering. It likes plenty of light, but cannot tolerate full sun. The compost must not be allowed to dry out.
To get the maximum benefit from this plant, it is advisable to keep it fairly cool and remove the faded flowers regularly.

Previous page: Cytisus x racemosus

Left: Euphorbia pulcherrima

Exacum affine

Gardenia

ORIGIN: China

The lovely, creamy-white double flowers of *Gardenia jasminoides* fill the air with the most wonderful fragrance. They really stand out against the glossy dark green foliage of this sturdy little shrub.

CARE

The gardenia likes a light, warm position with high humidity. The plant is a lime-hater so you should water it with soft rainwater (or boiled water) at room temperature. Use an acid, humus-rich compost for repotting. Never allow the compost to dry out during the summer, and water less during the plant's winter dormancy period, when it should be kept at a temperature of about 15°C (60°F).

The plant can go out into a shady spot in the garden during the summer. If it gets leggy, cut it back in the early spring.

Ixora (flame of the woods)

ORIGIN: China to India

Whereas once upon a time you needed a heated greenhouse to grow *Ixora coccinea*, crosses have now produced splendid hybrids that make excellent house plants.

The large clusters of flowers can be white, yellow, apricot, pink, scarlet or brick red. The evergreen leaf is a glossy dark green with a slightly leathery feel.

CARE

This plant is not one for the novice since it requires heat (20-22oC, 68-72oF) and high humidity. Mist regularly or stand the plant on an upturned

Following page: Ixora coccinea

Exacum affine

Below: Gardenia jasminoides

Ixora coccinea

very light position (southwest). In this case you must take care to keep the humidity up. This means you will either have to mist frequently or stand the plant on an upturned saucer in a tray of water. Keep the compost moist at all times and feed once every two weeks. Reduce watering in winter, when the plant should be kept cooler (10-15°C, 50-60°F). You can cut it back in spring.

Medinilla
ORIGIN: Philippines
The species name of *Medinilla* is *magnifica*, which tells us that one or more parts of the plant are large.
The winged stems bear large, leathery leaves. Similarly large, pendent flower heads with nu-

Following page: Medinilla magnifica

Below: Jacobinia carnea

saucer in a tray of water. The water you use for watering and misting must be softened. Feed with a weak solution of house plant fertilizer. Remove the faded flowers to encourage a second flush of blooms.
Overwinter the plant at a temperature of 15-18oC (60-65oF), and guard against cold and draughts.

Jacobinia (syn. Justicia, king's crown)
ORIGIN: Brazil
This bushy plant has flesh-pink to red flowers borne in large spikes on stalks above the foliage. The bracts, just visible between the flowers, are green to purple.
Jacobinia carnea usually flowers in summer and autumn, but you may some-times be able to buy one earlier in the season.
The deep veins give the leaves a jagged appearance.
CARE
This is not an easy plant to grow and it really does best in a heated greenhouse with high humidity.
If you grow it indoors, it needs warmth and a

Medinilla magnifica *flower*

Pentas (Egyptian star cluster)

ORIGIN: Arabia, tropical Africa and Madagascar

The flower umbels on this downy-leaved shrub appear at the tips of the shoots. There are around fifty species, but *Pentas lanceolata* is the one you are most likely to find. The colour of the flowers ranges from white to bright red and from light to deep pink and magenta.

CARE

This plant needs plenty of light but will not tolerate full sun. Keep the compost moist, use softened water, and add some house plant food to the water once a week. The humidity should be on the high side. Overwinter the plant at a temperature that does not drop below 12°C (55°F). Cut the plant back in the spring if necessary, and repot it in potting compost to which you have added some clay.

Medinilla magnifica *bud*

merous tiny pink flowers and large pink bracts develop at the ends of the stems. Its spreading habit and large leaves make it an unsuitable plant for a windowsill, but it will do very well on a pedestal close to the window.

CARE

Medinilla magnifica likes warmth and high humidity and would probably do best grown in a heated greenhouse. If you grow it indoors you will have to mist it regularly and, if possible, stand it on a bed of pebbles with water. It will need a great deal of water while in flower, and you should feed it with house plant fertilizer once every two weeks. Overwinter at about 15°C (60°F) and reduce the amount of water. Repot the plant in a free-draining, humus-rich potting compost.

Pentas lanceolata

Right: Primula obconica

Primula (poison primrose, fairy primrose, Chinese primrose)

ORIGIN: China and Europe

The poison primrose, *Primula obconica*, and the low-growing Chinese primrose, *P. sinensis* (syn. *P. praenitens*), cause an irritating skin rash in some people if they touch the hairy leaves. The white, pink, deep rose, salmon or blue flowers are borne in clusters on long stems. There are also beautiful bi-coloured varieties with a light edge shading to a deeper colour towards the centre. *P.o.* 'Achat', which shades from almost white to a deep pink, is a good example. The fairy primrose, *P. malacoides*, has small flowers arranged in tiers. Colours range from white to deep pink, and some varieties have a light edge to the petals. The common primrose, *P. acaulis* (syn. *P. vulgaris)* is to be found in the shops and garden centres in early spring.

Primula obconica *'Achat'*

Common primrose growing in the garden

The flowers, which come in a range of colours, are borne on short stems just above the leaf rosette.

CARE

Primulas like plenty of light but will not tolerate full sun. To prolong the flowering period try to keep them fairly cool. The common primrose can go out in the garden to overwinter, and will flower again the following spring. Keep the compost moist at all times.

The common primrose prefers to be slightly wetter, and the Chinese primrose drier. Feed with half-strength house plant fertilizer while the plants are in flower.

Primula acaulis

Below: Primula malacoides

Rhipsalodopsis (Easter cactus)

ORIGIN: Southern Brazil

A forest cactus with leaf-like triangular to hexagonal segmented stems that are erect then pendent. As the common name indicates, it blooms in spring, around Easter time. The fragrant red flowers of *Rhipsalodopsis gaertneri*, the most frequently-grown form, develop at the tips of the last stem segments.

CARE

If you buy a plant that is already in flower, put it in a light place, out of the sun. Do not turn the plant after this or the buds will drop. Keep the compost just moist during flowering and feed with house plant fertilizer once a month. Once the plant has finished flowering, put it in a shady

Left: Primula obconica *'Apple Blossom'*

spot in the garden and protect it from slugs. Bring it indoors again in the autumn and over-winter it at 10-15°C (50-60°F). Do not water it until the first buds start to show. Don't worry if you see the 'leaves' are shrivelling; it is the lack of moisture that stimulates the plant to form buds.

Saintpaulia (African violet)

ORIGIN: Tanzania

A very popular, easy house plant with attractive violet-shaped flowers that come in a range of colours: from white to pink and carmine, and from light blue to dark purple, sometimes with a light edge. There are also double and miniature varieties. The long-stemmed, downy leaves form a rosette. Growers are constantly trying to come up with something new, and by means of a complicated process they have developed African

Rhipsalidopsis gaertneri

Below: Rhipsalidopsis gaertneri

Schlumbergera truncatus

Following pages: Saintpaulia ionantha *hybrid*

violets with bi-coloured flowers-the 'Chimera group'. However, do not try to propagate these from leaf cuttings because you will not get the two-tone effect (white with another colour) in the offspring.

CARE

Give the African violet a light position out of the sun. What makes it such an easy plant is its love of warmth. Keep the compost moist at all times and feed with house plant fertilizer once a month. Water with tepid, preferably softened water. Always remove faded flowers. The plant will flower all year round provided you give it additional light in the winter. If the plant develops lot of foliage but few flowers, the problem could be the fertilizer. In this case use a low nitrogen fertilizer and remove some of the leaves. African violets are easy to propagate by means of leaf cuttings (a leaf plus a small piece of stem). They will root at a temperature of 20-25°C, 68-77°F). Do not mist African violets since drops of water on the hairy leaves can cause brown spots.

Schlumbergera (Christmas cactus)

ORIGIN: Brazil

This forest cactus is very like the Easter cactus, and it also has soft, trailing stems with flat, fleshy segments. The Christmas cactus blooms in winter, bearing red to lilac flowers at the ends of the young shoots. The petals are strongly reflexed.

CARE

The *Schlumbergera* (syn. *Zygocactus)* needs a period of drought in order to form buds. The plant needs to be kept cool ((12-15°C, 55-60°F)

Above and right: Senecio *Cruentus Group*

Below: a box of senecio plants

Senecio (cineraria)

ORIGIN: Canary Islands

The *Senecio* Cruentus group are compact plants, better known by their old name of cineraria. They have almost circular leaves with crinkled edges, surrounding a dense mass of flowers borne on a branched stem. There is a wide range of colours and shades-only a true orange and yellow are missing.

The flowers can be self-coloured, or have a white eye or white border.

Torenia fournieri

for about three months before flowering. Do not allow the stems to shrivel. Once the first flower buds start to show, gradually increase the water and move the plant to a warmer spot. Give it another rest period after flowering and put it outside at the end of May. Feed with a special cactus fertilizer every week. Bring the plant back indoors in August, put it in a cool spot and give it very little water. Like the Easter cactus, this cactus will drop its flower buds if it is turned in relation to the light source.

CARE

Give this plant plenty of light, but not too much sun. Never let the compost dry out, but take care not to waterlog it either. Try to keep the compost evenly moist. If the plant starts to droop for lack of water, stand it in a bowl of tepid water for half an hour. Aphids and whitefly can be a problem if the plant is standing in a draught. There is no point in keeping the plant once it has finished flowering.

Torenia

ORIGIN: Vietnam

Torenia fournieri is an attractive little annual with foxglove-like flowers in white, pink, blue or purple with white markings and a yellow throat.

CARE

This plant likes plenty of light and a fair amount of sun, but a south-facing window is too hot for it. A cool position will ensure the longest possible flowering period. The plant will benefit from a spell outside in the summer. Always keep the compost moist. Discard the plant on the compost heap after flowering, since this is an annual.

Stephanotis floribunda

Veltheimia

Suitable climbing and trailing plants

These climbing and trailing plants can be used in a window facing east or west:
• weeping Chinese lantern *(Abutilon megapotanicum)*
• lipstick vine *(Aeschynanthus)*
• glory bower *(Clerodendrum)*
• goldfish plant *(Columnea)*
• Indian strawberry *(Duchesnea)*
• wax plant *(Hoya)*
• Cape leadwort *(Plumbago)*
• Madagascar jasmine *(Stephanotis)*

Suitable bulbs, corms and rhizomes

These bulbs and corms will do well in an east or west-facing position:
• hot water plant *(Achimenes)*
• paintbrush *(Haemanthus)*
• gloxinia *(Sinningia)*
• forest lily *(Veltheimia)*

CHAPTER 3

A north-facing windowsill

There are a great many foliage plants that enjoy plenty of light but do not like direct sun, and there are some flowering plants that are equally happy in these conditions. The best place for them is a window facing north, east or, in some cases, west. In this chapter we look at the real shade-lovers. In the wild many of these plants grow under trees or bushes or on the fringes of a tropical rainforest.

Spathiphyllum patinii

Anthurium (painter's palette and flamingo flower)

ORIGIN: Central America

The cultivars of *Anthurium andreanum* and *A. scherzerianum* bear magnificent flowers (actually spathes surrounding a long spadix) which will provide colour for months on end. They come in bright red, orange, pink and white, as well as white with red spots. The anthuriums you are most likely to find in the shops are cultivars of *A. andreanum*. The growers have recently introduced compact hybrids with small, attractive flowers-the 'lady line'. 'Lady Jane' is a particularly pretty deep pink form.

CARE

Anthuriums like warm surroundings with relatively high humidity. Keep the compost moist, and use softened tepid water. Feed with a flowering house plant fertilizer every other week in summer. Put the plant in a slightly cooler spot (15-18°C, 60-65°F) for about two months in the winter, and reduce the amount of water. Repot in a humus-rich potting compost or one especially formulated for anthuriums.

Left: Anthurium

Anthurium

Below: Anthurium andreanum *'Lady Jane'*

Calceolaria (slipper flower)

ORIGIN: cool, mountainous areas in South America

The curious, pouch-like flowers cluster closely together in short spikes. The 'slippers' are usually yellow, but you should also be able to find orange, red and bronze cultivars, usually with spots in a contrasting colour. This plant is usually grown as an annual and you can discard it once it has finished flowering. The large-flowered varieties (*Calceolaria* x *herbeohybrida*) make the best house plants; the small, usually yellow-flowered slipper flowers are better as bedding plants in the garden.

CARE

Since the slipper flower will bloom for one season only, it is best to buy the plant in spring. Put it in a cool spot. Keep the compost moist at all times and remove the flowers as they fade. Beware of draughts, since this will encourage aphids and whitefly.

Above and below: Calceolaria

Clivia (kaffir lily)

ORIGIN: Natal

An old-fashioned evergreen that is currently enjoying renewed popularity. The glossy, leathery strap-like leaves are borne in a double row, and the sturdy stem emerges from the centre, carrying a cluster of lovely red or orange trumpet-shaped flowers.

The cultivars with variegated leaves need more light.

CARE

Clivia miniata is a very tough flowering plant, which is tolerant of the dry air in the house. It needs a period of rest from October onwards in order to form flower buds, so put it in a cool place (8-10°C, 45-50°F) and water very sparingly. The flower stalk will appear after a few months. Do not increase the water until the stalk is about 10 cm (4 inches) long. If you start watering before this, you will stop the growth. You can now move the plant to a warmer spot and feed weekly with a house plant fertilizer. Do not turn the plant while it is in flower or it will drop its buds. Only repot when the plant is actually pushing out of its existing pot.

Below and right: Clivia miniata

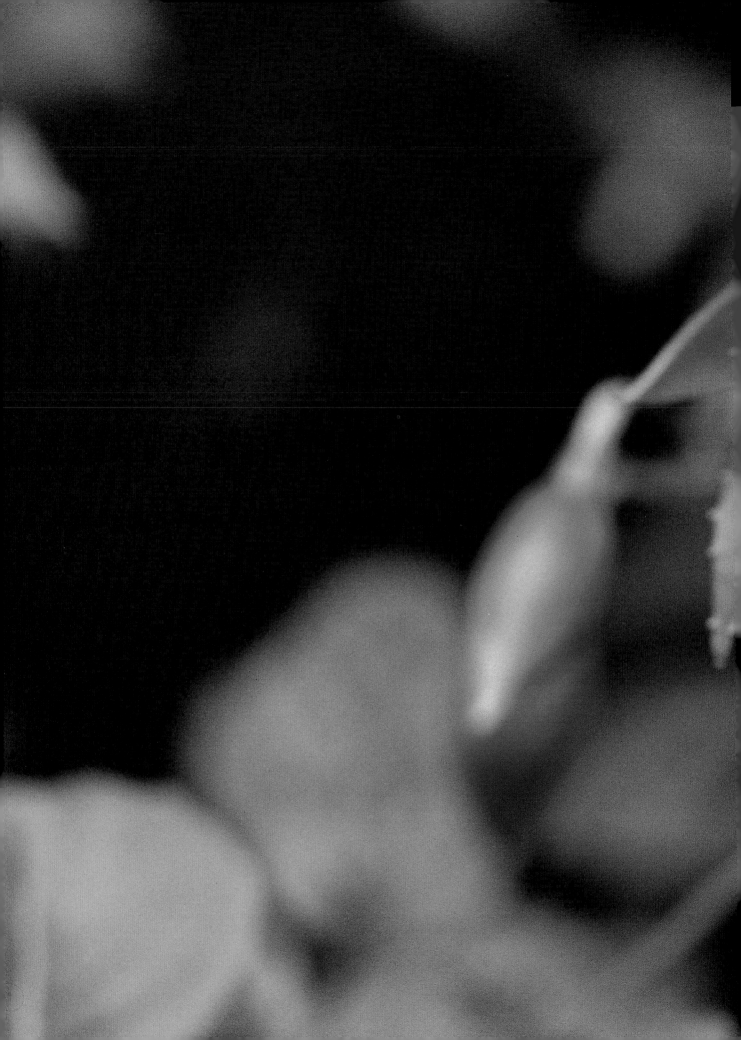

Fuchsia (lady's eardrops)

ORIGIN: South America, New Zealand, Haiti
The fuchsia is an immensely popular plant: there are numerous books devoted to it and fuchsia associations exist in countries all over the world. Fuchsias bloom profusely all summer long, displaying their usually pendent flowers in a wonderful palette of colours and shades. The flowers of the various hybrids range from slender and tubular to plump and frilly, in a single colour or bi-coloured. You can buy them as little more than seedlings and as substantial bushy plants. They are also available as standards. Fuchsias can be kept going for many years with the right care, although in time they will grow into patio plants. There are so many named varieties that it is impossible to list them all here.

Previous pages: Fuchsia 'Alison Ryle'

Fuchsia *'Gift Wrap'*

Below: Fuchsia 'Sunray'; right: Fuchsia 'Multa'

A fuchsia grown as a container plant

Below: Fuchsia *'Jubilee Waltz'*

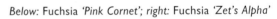

Fuchsia

Below: Fuchsia *'Pink Cornet'; right:* Fuchsia *'Zet's Alpha'*

CARE

Fuchsias like a bright, shady position. Keep the compost moist. Feed them once every two weeks. Small plants can be kept in a cool place indoors or put outside in a planter. Larger specimens are best treated as patio plants. They must be brought inside before the first night frost and can be cut back immediately. You can also prune them in early March. The temperature must not be allowed to drop below 5°C (40°F) during the winter. Water very occasionally since the soil should never be allowed to dry out completely. The plants can go back outside again around the middle of May.

Below: Fuchsia 'Welsh Dragon'

Previous pages: Fuchsias grown as climbing plants

Hydrangea macrophylla

Hydrangea

ORIGIN: East Asia, North and South America

Hydrangea macrophylla is a well-known and deservedly popular shrub. It is sold as a flowering house plant from spring onwards, with large flower heads in blue, soft lilac, pink or white.

Teller type hydrangeas-usually referred to as lacecaps-are particularly sought-after at the moment. They have dense clusters of tiny fertile flowers in the centre, surrounded by a coronet of much larger, sterile flowers. There is also a new variety *(H. macrophylla* 'Uzu') with bowl-shaped, recurved petals that are not unlike lilac blossom.

CARE

Strictly speaking hydrangeas belong in the garden, but they are forced to do duty as pot plants. Put the plant in the coolest possible position in the house and water daily with softened tepid water.

Hydrangea macrophylla, *Teller type*

If the flowers start to wilt, stand the pot in tepid water for an hour or so. You can put the plant out in the garden at the end of May. Feed once every two weeks during the summer. The blue of the flowers is artificial. Growers give white or pink hydrangeas alum, which makes the flowers turn blue.

You can buy alum from the chemist. Rusting iron will also bring about interesting colour changes.

Impatiens walleriana *hybrid*

Impatiens *New Guinea Group*

Impatiens (busy Lizzie)

ORIGIN: tropical East Africa

Can there be anyone who does not know the busy Lizzie with its flat flowers in almost every conceivable colour except yellow and blue? There are also bi-coloured forms. The double-flowered varieties resemble little roses. We usually plant this attractive plant *(Impatiens walleriana)*, grown as an annual, in the garden or in planters outside. In recent years, we have been able to buy hybrids of *Impatiens hawkeri*, the New Guinea group, which are sturdier and stronger in every way. These varieties often have dark green or bronze foliage.

CARE

This fleshy little plant likes plenty of light but not too much sun, so an east-facing windowsill is also a possible position for it. Busy Lizzies need a lot of water and you should feed them once every two weeks. If you remove the dead flower heads regularly, they will go on blooming throughout the summer. You can overwinter them, but the plants tend to become drawn and leggy and the flowers generally deteriorate. They are extremely easy to propagate by means of stem cuttings in spring. Simply put the cutting in a glass of water and wait until roots form before planting it up in ordinary potting compost. Once your new plant starts to grow, pinch it back several times to create a good, bushy plant.

Rhododendron (Japanese azalea, Indian azalea)

ORIGIN: China and Taiwan

There are two species of rhododendron that earn a place on the windowsill: the cultivars of *Rhododendron obtusum* (Japanese azalea) and *R. simsii* (Indian azalea). These are their official names, but we tend to lump them all together as azaleas. They are evergreen shrubs which flower readily. The Japanese azalea blooms profusely, bearing single flowers ranging from pink to lilac. There is also one which has brick red flowers. The most commonly found type is the Indian azalea, which has much larger flowers that can be single, semi-double or double in colours ranging from pure white to deep red. There are one or two varieties with magenta or yellow flowers.

Rhododendrons in the Royal Conservatories in Laken, Holland

An azalea of the Simsii Group

CARE

Keep the plant as cool as possible. Azaleas will flourish in a heated room, but the flowering period will be much shorter. Keep the compost moist at all times and water with softened, lime-free water, preferably in the saucer or cache pot. You can mist the plant while it is not in flower, since it likes a humid atmosphere. It is also a good idea to plunge the pot up to the rim in a bowl of water once a week. Under no circumstances should you feed an azalea. After flowering re-move the dead heads, pinch back the young shoots and put the plant in a cool place. After the middle of May, plunge the plant, pot and all, into the soil in the garden, in a partially shady spot. Make sure that the soil around the root ball remains moist. In the autumn, just before the first frost, bring the plant back indoors and put it in a cool, bright place. Once the azalea comes into flower again you can bring it into the living room.

Spathiphyllum (peace lily)

ORIGIN: Colombia

This plant has large, long, dark green leaves on long stalks that grow directly out of the compost. The flowers (in fact a spathe around a spadix) are borne on long stems above the leaves. The spathe, which curves attractively around the

cream-coloured spadix, is pure white, gradually shading to green as the flower ages. The flowers resemble those of the anthurium, which is not surprising since they belong to the same family. There are a number of cultivars of *Spathiphyllum walisii*, which vary considerably in height and in the size of the leaves and flowers. *S. patinii* is smaller in every respect. These plants purify the air and can help relieve stress.

CARE

Like many shade-lovers, these plants like a humid atmosphere. This means that you will have to mist them a great deal. You can also stand them on a tray of moist gravel. This is essential if they are in a place where hot air circulates. Keep the compost moderately moist and feed once every two weeks while the plant is in flower. Always use softened water at room temperature. The plant can be kept a little cooler in winter, but the temperature must not be allowed to drop below 15°C (60°F).

Streptocarpus (Cape primrose)

ORIGIN: South Africa

A very attractive flowering plant with large,

An azalea as a container plant

trumpet-shaped flowers and long, deeply-veined leaves. 'Constant Nymph', with its purple-blue flowers has always been a very popular cultivar, but crosses have meant that nowadays we can buy plants with pink, white, blue or carmine flowers, all of which have darker streaks on the throat.

CARE

This plant will also do well on an east-facing windowsill. If it is looked after properly it will flower all summer long. Make sure that the compost never dries out and feed with house plant fertilizer every other week. Remove faded flowers and any leaves that are looking tatty. The plant needs a rest period in winter, when you should put it in a cool place (13-15°C, 55-60°F). Water sparingly during this period. Repot the plant in spring, move it to a warmer place and increase the amount of water.

Azalea

Suitable climbing and trailing plants

These climbing and trailing plants thrive in a north-facing window:
- goldfish plant *(Columnea)*
- wax plant *(Hoya)*

Suitable bulbs, corms and rhizomes

There a very few bulbs that do well on a north-facing windowsill, but the autumn crocus *(Colchicum)* is an exception.

Spathiphyllum *'Mozart'*

Streptocarpus

CHAPTER 4

Flowering trailing and climbing plants

Trailing plants have long, lax stems or shoots that cannot support themselves and grow flat along the ground or, if they are suspended from a height, trail decoratively. If these stems encounter an obstacle they will creep up it and behave very much like a climber. A climber, by contrast, clings on with tendrils, aerial roots or suckers, or twines itself around other plants, a pole or a wire. In the wild they can grow up all sorts of different plants and create an impenetrable mass of stems and foliage. In the house, we have to help the plants by providing them with wires stretched along the wall, or with a moss pole or cane for support. We can also let them grow up through another plant.

Foliage plants can provide support for flowering climbers

Using trailing and climbing plants

Flowering climbers with leggy growth can use a sturdy, bushy house plant to scramble through. You could also plant one of these climbers in the same pot as a tall foliage plant, so that the foliage plant is bedecked with the climber's flowers.

If you decide to try this, you must make sure that the plants you choose have the same requirements in terms of light and water.

As far as trailing plants are concerned, it is important to remember that they can suffer considerably from the hot air rising from central heating, and these plants should be misted regularly while the heating is on. Make sure, too, that the compost in the pot never dries out. A trailing plant on the windowsill has a particularly difficult time of it in the winter, especially if the trailing stems are actually in contact with the radiator.

It is much better not to stand trailing plants on the windowsill. Instead, hang them at a reasonable height. There are some very strong species which will find the living room too warm. They will do best in a window in a cooler bedroom or perhaps in a porch.

Abutilon (weeping Chinese lantern)

ORIGIN: Southern Brazil

Abutilon megapotamicum has velvety, pointed leaves with serrated edges, borne on long, lax shoots. The pendent flowers are very striking; yellow petals and almost black stamens protrude from the red, bell-shaped calyx.

The variegated-leaf form is the most widely grown. When you buy it, it will probably be tied up. If you untie the stems, you can treat this plant as a climber and let it grow up a support in the conservatory.

CARE

This plant likes plenty of light and will even tolerate full sun. Never let the compost dry out, and feed with house plant fertilizer every two weeks. The abutilon also makes a very good container plant for the patio.

Abutilon megapotamicum

Aeschynanthus (lipstick vine)

ORIGIN: Southeast Asia

The lipstick vine is a trailing plant with long, lax stems and glossy, dark green, fleshy leaves.

Clusters of flowers appear at the tips of the stems. *Aeschynanthus lobbianus* is the most frequently cultivated variety. The flowers have a very long dark calyx, covered with downy hairs, from which tubular scarlet flowers emerge. There are all sorts of attractive cultivars, including 'Ara', with red edges to the leaves, 'Mira', and 'Mona Lisa', which has shorter, darker flowers.

CARE

This plant needs a lot of light but dislikes direct sunlight. A window facing north or east suits it very well. It likes to be warm, but in winter, when it needs to rest for about two months, it is better to keep it at a temperature of 10-15°C (50-60°F).

By giving the plant this time in cooler conditions you will stimulate the formation of flower buds.

Make sure that the compost is always reasonably moist, except during the dormant period. Mist regularly with softened water, because the lipstick vine enjoys high humidity.

Feed with a low-nitrogen fertilizer once every two weeks during the growing season. If necessary, repot in a humus-rich compost after the dormant period.

Allamanda

ORIGIN: Brazil

Allamanda cathartica is a fast-growing climber with glossy, dark green foliage and golden-yellow trumpet-shaped flowers borne in clusters. This plant is better suited to the greenhouse or conservatory than the living room, since it enjoys a fairly humid environment and this is difficult to provide indoors, particularly in the winter.

Left: Aechynanthus *'Mira'*

Below: Allamanda cathartica

Bougainvillea glabra *hybrid*

CARE

This plant likes plenty of light, but cannot tolerate full sun. It does not have a dormant period, which means that it does not have to be kept cool in the winter (in fact, the temperature should not be allowed to drop below 18°C (65°F), and it will not drop its leaves.

Keep the compost moist at all times and feed with a house plant fertilizer occasionally. Obviously this plant needs a lot of misting, but take care during the flowering period since drops of water can cause unsightly spots on the flowers.

Bougainvillea (paper flower)

ORIGIN: Brazil

Bougainvillea glabra is a strong climber familiar to us from Mediterranean holidays where we see it growing over white-painted walls.

The insignificant tubular flowers, which range from sulphur yellow to white, rapidly drop, but the papery bracts, in groups of three, remain on the plant for a very long time. It is these deep purple, magenta or pink bracts that make the plant so decorative.

Nowadays you will also find varieties with white, orange, red, pink and apricot bracts. There is also a compact, bushy purple variety known as 'Purple Dwarf'. The plant climbs by hooking itself on with its strong spines. If there is nothing for the bougainvillea to climb up, it will form a dense bush with branches that creep along the ground.

CARE

This is a real sun-lover that can climb to 4 or 5 metres (13 to 16 feet) high. It can also be grown as a container plant for the patio and enjoys spending the summer outside in a sheltered, sunny spot.

It needs a lot of water when it is growing and flowering, and should be fed with house plant fertilizer every week. In the winter, when the plant is not looking its best, it should be put in a cool place at about 5-10°C (40-50°F). Water very sparingly indeed and do not feed the plant at all. The plant will lose a lot of leaves during this period and can be pruned when it starts back into growth. In the late spring, once the new shoots are several inches long, reduce the amount of water for several weeks to encourage flower buds to form, but take care not to let the young shoots dry out.

Clerodendrum (glory bower)

ORIGIN: West Africa

A climber with dark green, heart-shaped leaves. The flowers are borne in clusters on stems that grow out from the leaf axils. The cream-coloured calyx lasts for a long time, gradually changing colour through green to a dark pinky red. The scarlet petals rapidly drop, leaving the striking stamens.

Clerodendrum x *speciosum* is not usually sold as a climber, but as a dwarfed flowering plant. This is because it has been pinched out several times and treated with a growth inhibitor. The effect will wear off after a while, and the plant will start to produce climbing stems up to 4 metres (13 feet) long.

CARE

Put the glory bower in full light in a coolish place. It needs some sunlight, so a window facing east or west would be a good choice. Once it has finished flowering, move it to a greenhouse or conservatory where it can grow out. During the winter, when it needs a time of rest, water very infrequently. The temperature should be around 12°C (55°F). Most of the leaves will drop. Replace the potting compost in spring and cut back any overlong shoots.

Bougainvillea against the backdrop of the Mediterranean

Bougainvillea spectabilis *hybrid*

If possible, give the plant a short day treatment to stimulate bud formation. It should not have more than nine hours of light a day.

Keep the compost moist while the plant is growing and flowering, and feed it every two weeks.

Columnea (goldfish plant)

ORIGIN: Central America

A plant with supple trailing stems that can grow to over a metre (3 feet) long, covered over the whole length with small, almost round, downy leaves with a gold sheen. It blooms in early summer, with long, orange-red, tubular flowers emerging from the leaf axils of the newly formed stems. *Columnea microphylla* 'Stavanger' has

Left: white bougainvillea

Below: Columnea hirta *'Susan'*

Following pages: Clerodendrum thomsoniae

slightly larger leaves and flowers and can, like the species, flower very profusely. The variegated cultivar with yellow-splashed leaves is called 'Hostag'. Yet another variety is *Columnea hirta*, which has stems up to 70 centimetres (about $2^1/_2$ feet) long and very hairy, long oval leaves.

CARE

These plants like a great deal of light but will not tolerate any sun. Exposure to sun will cause scorch marks, particularly in the varieties with hairy leaves. This plant originates from tropical rainforests, which means that it needs high humidity. Plants with hairy leaves should not be sprayed, so you should put them in a cache pot and then stand that in a saucer filled with water. Even better is to hang the plant in a humid environment.

Keep the compost moderately moist at all times in the summer and always use tepid water. Cut the plant back after flowering. If you want to be sure of flowers again next year, give the plant a winter rest by putting it in a cooler place (12-

Fruit of Columnea *'Hostag'*

Below: Columnea *'Hostag'*

Columnea microphylla

15°C, 55-60°F) and watering less. In spring, pot the goldfish plant on in slightly acid potting compost.

Hoya (wax plant and miniature wax plant)

ORIGIN: Southern China to Australia

Hoya carnosa is a twining house plant with very dark green foliage. The delicate pink flowers are very pretty and strongly scented. They hang in clusters on supple stems. The common name 'wax plant' refers to the texture and sheen of the flowers. Thick drops of sticky nectar, which taste deliciously sweet, often form on the pendent flowers, and this explains the hoya's other common name of 'honey plant'. Take care that the nectar does not leave marks on your furniture. There is also a variegated variety ('Variegata') of this hoya and one which has a curled leaf that is light on the back, 'Compacta'. *H. bella,* the miniature wax plant, is smaller in all respects and has a narrow leaf. This plant also has pendent flower clusters. The flowers are white with an inner ring of violet petals at the centre. Although *H. carnosa* is a climber, *H. bella* is usually treated as a hanging plant.

CARE

H. carnosa likes to be kept quite cool, but the temperature should not drop below 10°C (50°F). It also needs plenty of light, but avoid full sun or the leaves will discolour. The plant will produce fewer flower buds if it does not get enough light. A window facing east, west or north is suitable. Once the plant is in bud do not turn it or the buds will drop.

Keep the compost moist in the summer, but reduce the amount of water in winter while the plant is in a cool place. You can actually allow the compost to get quite dry. Mist regularly while the plant is growing and feed with house plant fertilizer every two weeks.

Ipomoea (morning glory)

ORIGIN: Central Asia

This climber appears in the shops and garden centres around mid-April. As it twines its way around a cane or climbs through another plant, the morning glory works its way upwards. This annual, with its light green, heart-shaped leaves and trumpet flowers, which open early in the morning and close again in the afternoon, is a real beauty. Each flower only lasts one day, but with good care you should be able to get a constant succession of buds.

CARE

Ipomoea purpurea and *I. tricolor* are annuals that really prefer to be out in the garden, but will

Hoya bella

Hoya carnosa 'Compacta'

Below: Ipomoea 'Heavenly Blue'

grow in the house. They want a warm, light position and will happily take full sun. Water them freely and feed with house plant fertilizer every week.

If you want the plant to climb, you will have to give it something to climb up-netting, another plant or string. You can also train it up one of the preformed wire shapes that are so fashionable at the moment. You should be able to find them in your local garden centre. This plant is easy to raise from seed.

Jasminum (jasmine)
ORIGIN: Central Asia
Jasminum officinale and *J. polyanthum* are shrubs with very long stems that have to be tied

Right: jasmine

Below: Ipomoea purpurea

in. The long clusters of starry white flowers have a delightful fragrance.

The composite leaf has five or more fine lobes. *J. officinale* is generally finer than *J. polyanthum* (Chinese jasmine). The leaves will drop in the winter.

CARE

This strong climber prefers a cool position. The temperature can go as low as a degree or two above freezing in winter, and in the warmer parts of the country the plant will grow quite happily in the garden.

It likes full sun, but in mid-summer it can get too hot behind glass and does better outside. Always keep the compost really moist and feed once every two weeks while the plant is growing and flowering.

Mist it regularly as well. Keep the plant cool in winter, reduce the water and do not feed. Cut back hard in early spring.

Mandevilla boliviensis

Left: Mandevilla laxa

Below: Mandevilla 'Aphrodite'

Mandevilla (syn. Dipladenia)

ORIGIN: South America

Mandevilla or pink allamanda (which is usually sold under its old name of *Dipladenia)* is a twining plant with long stems and glossy green foliage. The trumpet-shaped flowers are borne in clusters at the tips of the stems or in the leaf axils. There are several varieties: *Mandevilla laxa,* like *M. boliviensis,* has white flowers. There are also varieties and hybrids with pink, lilac or red flowers. They bloom on the young stems.

CARE

This plant is usually fairly small when you buy it, but in the right spot it can grow to an impressive size so will probably do best in a conservatory or greenhouse. It needs a light position with protection against the full heat of the midday sun. A west-facing window is ideal, although the plant would also thrive in a window facing east. It can go outside in the summer. Give it plenty of water and feed it every two weeks.

This climber needs to be kept cooler in winter (at about 10°C, 50°F) and you should water very sparingly at this time. Prune the plant in spring to keep it bushy and prevent it from flowering at the top only.

Passiflora (passion flower)

ORIGIN: Brazil and Central America

Passiflora caerulea is a climber with sturdy, deeply lobed leaves. The tendrils will cling tenaciously to anything within reach. The flowers are about 10 cm (4 inches) across and extremely striking. The fifty or more needle-like petals, which are almost black at the base, white in the middle and a beautiful purple at the tip, stand out against the greenish-white calyx. The dark,

Passiflora *x* alato-caerulea

Passiflora antioquensis

Passiflora subpeltata

cruciform anther and pistils protrude from the centre of the flower. *P. caerulea* is not the only form available. You should also be able to find passion flowers in other colours, such as *Passiflora* x *alato-caerulea*, a variety that has very large flowers with a deep pink calyx and purple petals, and *P.* 'Victoria', which has pink, re-curved petals.

The white-flowered *P. subpeltata* is also ex-tremely attractive. These varieties are not as hardy and will not survive a frost. They should not be exposed to temperatures below 5°C (40°F). If the passion flower is pollinated it will produce large, plum-shaped fruits, some of which are edible.

CARE

The passion flower is a rampant climber and can sometimes outgrow its welcome in the living room, so you would probably be wise to put it in a greenhouse or conservatory. *P. caerulea* can grow in a sheltered spot outdoors, against a south-facing wall. From this you can tell that this plant prefers it cool and can tolerate a certain amount of frost in winter. Indoors, the passion flower prefers a position out of the full sun, and is happiest on a windowsill facing east or west. It is difficult to keep a passion flower in good heart

all year round in a centrally heated house-in winter, in particular, it will lose a lot of its leaves. You can cut the plant back hard in the spring, to 6 or 8 leaf nodes. In summer, make sure that the compost never dries out and feed with house plant fertilizer once every two weeks.

Passiflora edulis

Passiflora foetida

Plumbago (Cape leadwort)

ORIGIN: South Africa

A shrub with vigorous climbing stems that have no difficulty clinging to a cane or wire.

The sky-blue flowers are borne in downy clusters on the young shoots.

There is also a white cultivar of *P. auriculata*, known as 'Alba'. The red-flowered *P. indica* is rarely available to buy.

CARE

The red-flowered plumbago likes a warm position and insists on high humidity. The more familiar *P. auriculata* is a climber that needs a lot of light but has to be protected against really strong sun.

In summer it enjoys a spell outside in a sheltered spot out of the sun. Because the plant prefers to be treated as a patio plant and consequently has to be moved twice a year, it is a good idea to tie the long shoots in to a sturdy wire frame anchored in the pot. Bring your plumbago indoors and put it in a slightly heated place where it stays cool in winter (at least 5°C, 40°F). Always keep the compost moist during the growing period and feed with house plant fertilizer once every two weeks.

Water sparingly in winter and do not feed the plant at all. Cut the plant back at this time, too, to encourage the growth of plenty of new flowering shoots in spring. Give the plant fresh compost in spring, and pot it on into a larger container if necessary. After this, start increasing the water gradually.

Stephanotis (Madagascar jasmine)

ORIGIN: Madagascar

This familiar favourite, once widely used in bridal bouquets, is a twining vine with glossy, dark green leaves setting off the heavily-scented, waxy white flowers.

CARE

Although I have seen this plant growing in full sun among the rocks on Madagascar's east coat, *Stephanotis floribunda* is less than happy to sit in full sun on a windowsill. It does, however, like bright light.

When you buy stephanotis, choose a plant with plenty of flower buds, the first few of which are just starting to open. This is important, because it is very difficult to get the plant to flower the first year yourself.

Stephanotis must be kept in a cool place in winter (12-15°C, 55-60°F) in order to form buds. It needs virtually no water during this period. Prune it in the early spring so that it can form

Plumbago auriculata

Plumbago auriculata *'Alba'*

plenty of new shoots on which the flower clusters can develop. Once the first flower buds appear, it is time to increase the amount of water and raise the temperature slightly. The plant must remain in the same position relative to the light source or it will drop its buds. Keep the compost moist at all times during the growing season and mist regularly with softened water. Stephanotis is susceptible to cold, so make sure the plant is well wrapped-up when you buy it if the weather is bad.

Thunbergia (black-eyed Susan)

ORIGIN: Southeast Africa

A down-covered climber with bright green leaves and cheerful single flowers which are yellow, orange or white with a dark eye in the centre –

Stephanotis floribunda

Plumbago indica

Below: Stephanotis *growing among the rocks on Madagascar*

Thunbergia alata 'Alba'

Right: Thunbergia alata

hence the common name. The white cultivar of this annual climber, *Thunbergia alta,* is called 'Alba'.

CARE

This plant likes lots of light and will even tolerate some sun. It can go outside in summer, when it will bloom profusely. Indoors, you can grow it through a sturdy evergreen house plant or on a trellis or netting. Keep the compost moist and feed with house plant fertilizer every other week. Once the plant has finished flowering at the end of the summer you can discard it.

Outdoors, where insects can pollinate the flowers, the plant will set seed that you can sow the following spring. The results can be disappointing, however, so it is probably safer to buy fresh seed.

CHAPTER 5

Bulbs, corms and rhizomes

In the dark winter months, many people look forward eagerly to spring, when the first cheerful bulbs start to appear-tulips, hyacinths, daffodils and the lovely, smaller species like crocuses, grape hyacinths, irises and snowdrops. Many of these bulbs are available in the shops, ready potted up and already in bud. This is obviously the easiest and quickest way to get some colour on your windowsill, but there is no reason why you should not start your bulbs off for yourself.

Right: Oxalis regnellii

Below: Hippeastrum

Snowdrops, the harbingers of spring

Grape hyacinths in the garden

Flowering bulbs and corms in the house

There are many bulbs, corms and rhizomes that can be grown as effectively indoors as they can in the garden. The garden varieties, which you can also grow indoors, generally need a cold period. Others are real house plants. Bulbs and corms that flower early in the year will not last as long in a warm room as they will outside in the cold, so you should put them in the coolest place you can find. There are also summer-flowering bulbs that will tolerate much more heat. These make good house plants and often also lend themselves to planting in a pot on the balcony or patio. The most obvious difference between bulbs and other house plants is the period of dormancy that bulbs must have. Once the flowers are finished you should gradually reduce the amount of water until the leaves have died down completely. The bulbs can then be put away, pot and all.

above the edge of the pot. Finish filling the pot with compost to just below the edge and press it down again. If you put the bulbs in the garden you do not need to water them. If you put them in a shed, unheated cellar or garage, they will have to have some water.

Growing in water

There are a few bulbs that can be grown in water – hyacinths, crocuses and 'Paperwhite' narcissi. For hyacinths you can buy the familiar hyacinth vases. For years they were almost impossible to find in the shops, but they have recently come back into fashion, and small children, in particular, find it fascinating to see how an apparently dead bulb gradually produces roots, a shoot, leaves and eventually a flower. Fill the hyacinth vase with water to just under the bottom of the bulb – no higher or the bulb will rot. Put it away in a cool, dark place, preferably not warmer than 10°C (50°F).

Left: the first bulbs can be in flower for Christmas

Below: crocuses grown in water

Hyacinths in water

The bulb will start by developing roots and then a shoot. Top up with water occasionally, but make sure the level remains below the base of the bulb.

When the shoot is about 7 cm (3 inches) long, you can bring the vase out of the dark and bring it into the house, in a light, slightly warmer place.

Of all the spring-flowering bulbs, the hyacinth, which is grown largely for its wonderful fragrance, can tolerate the greatest warmth. You can also buy crocus vases nowadays-miniature versions of the hyacinth vase-in which you can grow a crocus in exactly the same way.

The deliciously-scented white narcissus 'Paperwhite' can also be grown in water. Place the bulbs in a shallow container holding a layer of well-washed gravel. The bulbs should be submerged in the gravel to about half their depth. Make sure that there is enough room underneath for their roots and that the bulbs are not standing in water. This narcissus does not require a cold period nor does it have to be kept in the dark, so you can put the container straight on to the windowsill.

After flowering

Once the flowers have finished, put the bulbs in their pots in a cool, light spot and continue to water them for a while. Stop watering once the leaves have died back completely. When the weather permits, you can plant some-although not all-bulbs out in the garden: 'Paperwhite' narcissus stand no chance at all, while hyacinths will flower eventually but the blooms are likely to be much smaller. Bulbs sold for naturalization, such as snowdrops, grape hyacinths, cro-

Spring flowers on a plant table

Still life with bulbs

cuses, daffodils and narcissi, chionodoxa (glory of the snow) and the various species sold in pots, such as fritillaries, small anemones and lilies of the valley, will flower happily in the garden the following year. Botanical tulips will also flower again.

Ideas for the windowsill

Pots of flowering bulbs can simply be placed on the windowsill among the other plants. The flowers will show to best advantage against green foliage plants. Why not plant up a bowl with a few green plants and leave room for one or more pots of flowering bulbs? This creates a very elegant effect on the windowsill because you are not looking at a lot of different pots. Once the bulbs are over, you can take them out, pot and all, and replace them with another pot of bulbs. You can also cover the surface of the compost in a big bowl or container like this with moss. And for a simple but effective table decoration, take a bowl with a foot and place the bulbs among some decorative ivies.

Suitable bulbs, corms and rhizomes

The bulbs, corms and rhizomes described here do well when grown indoors.

Achimenes (hot water plant)
ORIGIN: Central America
A herbaceous, bushy plant with dark green leaves. Hybridization has produced plants with

Achimenes

Colchicum *will flower without soil or water*

flowers in wonderful shades of pink, carmine and purple. There is also a white-flowered cultivar.

CARE

Achimenes hybrids like to be kept moderately moist at all times while they are in flower. The plant hates cold water, so always use water at room temperature and add a liquid house plant fertilizer to it every two weeks. (Despite their common name, do not be tempted to give them hot water!)

These plants like high humidity and a light position, but no direct sun: a spot facing east, west or close to a north-facing window would be ideal. Achimenes have tiny tubers, known as tubercles. In autumn, when the plants start to look jaded, stop watering and let them die right back. During the dormant period the plants must be kept cool. In early spring, take the tubercles out of the pot and pot them up in fresh compost. Plant them about 2 cm (1 inch) deep in a light, acid compost with added peat and leaf mould. Gradually increase the water and move the pots to a light position once the first shoots show. Remember that these plants like high humidity, and guard against draughts.

Colchicum (autumn crocus)

ORIGIN: Central, Southern and Western Europe, North Africa

You can buy *Colchicum autumnalis* bulbs almost in flower in August. This bulb does not need potting up; you can simply place it among other plants on the windowsill or group several of them together in an attractive container. They will soon flower without your having to water them at all, producing large pinky-mauve flowers that resemble a large crocus. (Despite their common name, they are not in fact crocuses.) Once

they have finished flowering you can plant them out in the garden, where they will surprise you in spring with an imposing clump of quite large, dark green leaves. Take care if there are children around, since every part of this plant is poisonous.

Crocus

ORIGIN: the Jura mountains, the Alps, the Apennines and the Pyrenees

Several types of crocus are suitable for cultivation indoors, particularly the large-flowered cultivars *(Crocus vernus)*.

CARE

Pot crocuses up from October onwards and keep them dark and cool (about 9°C, 48°F) or plunge the pots into the soil in the garden. When the noses are well-developed and are at least 5 cm (2

Colchicum 'Lilac Wonder'

Large-flowered crocus

inches) long, bring the pots indoors and put them in a lighter place. After flowering, they can go out in a sunny to partially shaded spot in the garden.

Cyclamen

ORIGIN: eastern Mediterranean

This corm, which often has beautifully marked silver-grey leaves from which delicate, butterfly flowers in shades of white, pink and red rise on slender stems, is one of the most popular flowering house plants. There are also miniature forms that are truly delightful, although the range of colours is greater in the large-flowered varieties. There are also varieties with frilled flowers.

CARE

The plant likes plenty of light but will not tolerate direct sunlight. If you keep your cyclamen in a cool room (at about 15°C, 60°F), it will give you pleasure for a very long time. Water generously from the bottom, putting the water into the saucer or cache pot. Never water the compost from above since this can cause the crown to rot. An hour after watering, check the saucer or pot, and tip away any remaining water. Feed with a house plant fertilizer once every two weeks while the plant is growing and flowering. Yellow leaves and faded flowers should be twisted and pulled off the plant. Once the plant has finished flowering and the foliage starts to wilt,

Cyclamen persicum

progressively reduce the amount of water and stop feeding until all the leaves have turned yellow. Put the plant in its pot away in a cool place (10°C, 50°F). When new shoots start to show in the centre of the crown, take the corm out of the pot, clean it carefully, pot it up in fresh compost and gradually bring it into growth in a slightly warmer position.

Gloriosa (glory lily)

ORIGIN: tropical Asia and tropical Africa

Gloriosa rothschildiana is a climber with long, lax stems. The leaves terminate in a tendril with which the plant clings to a wire or string. The bright red flowers, usually with a yellow edge, grow from the leaf axils. The flower is composed of six reflexed, scalloped petals. The long stamens point down. Every part of the glory lily is poisonous.

CARE

This is a plant for a very light, but not too sunny position. Keep the compost moist, but not wet while the plant is growing. Feed every week with half-strength house plant fertilizer. Water with tepid water and remove the dead flowers as soon as they fade. Once flowering is over, gradually reduce the amount of water until the plant has died back. Put the tuber away in its pot at a temperature of about 10°C (50°F). In spring, remove the tuber from the pot very carefully (take great care not to damage the nose-if you do, you can throw the plant away there and then) and replant it horizontally at a depth of 5 cm (2 inches) in fresh compost to which you have added some loam and sharp sand. If the temperature is high enough, the first shoot will rapidly appear. The glory lily can be bought as a flowering plant. Tubers are generally only available from specialist growers.

Cyclamen persicum *with beautifully marked leaves*

Fringed cyclamen

Gloriosa rothschildiana

Gloriosa rothschildiana

Haemanthus (paintbrush, blood lily)

ORIGIN: Natal

Haemanthus multiflorus is the most common variety, but *Haemanthus albiflos* (paintbrush) is also available, particularly from specialist growers.

The short-stemmed leaves are lance-shaped. The spherical flower head measures 20 to 30 cm (8 to 12 inches) across and is composed of innumerable tiny, star-shaped red flowers with long stamens. The cultivar 'King Alfred' has salmon pink flowers.

CARE

You can buy the bulb in spring, when you should pot it up with the nose just under the surface of the compost. Put it in a warm place and water regularly, but take care not to overwater since bulbs are prone to rot.

In summer, when the plant is growing well, it will need more water and a feed of house plant fertilizer once every two weeks. It likes a bright position out of the sun.

After flowering, keep watering until the foliage turns yellow. Then put the plant and pot away at

Following page: Haementhus multiflorus

Below: Haementhus coccineus

about 12°C (55°F) so that it can become dormant. Bring it out again in spring, remove the bulb from the pot, clean it and repot it in fresh compost. You can also buy haemanthus as a flowering plant.

Hippeastrum (amaryllis)

ORIGIN: Central and South America

Although *Hippeastrum* is still referred to as amaryllis, the true amaryllis is really a plant for the garden, where it can be planted among the perennials or grown in a large pot on the patio. The *Hippeastrum* hybrid is an easy to grow bulb for indoor cultivation.

You can buy the bulbs from autumn until well into April. If you plant the bulb early enough, the flowers will appear by Christmas.

The size of the bulb determines the number of stalks and flowers: the larger the bulb, the more of these huge, velvety dark red, bright red, pink, salmon, white, red and white or pink and white flowers you will get.

The thick hollow stem can bear 3 to 5 flowers. There are also some very decorative small-flowered amaryllis, and specialist growers also sell

Amaryllis planted among foliage plants in a container

From bulb to bloom

Hippeastrum 'Papilio'

other varieties and cultivars with beautifully marked petals.

CARE

The bulb can be planted any time from the beginning of November onwards. It is important to avoid touching the roots and to damage them as little as possible. Put a layer of compost in the pot, place the bulb on it, add more compost and

A few weeks later, a flowering amaryllis amidst the greenery

shake the pot gently so that the compost can get in among the roots. Once the compost has been firmed down well, about one-third of the neck of the bulb should be protruding above the surface. Water, and then put the pot away in a cool place (about 15°C, 60°F).

Water regularly, but sparingly, because the bulb must not get too wet. The flower stalk will soon emerge. Once the first bud is visible, bring the pot into full light, perhaps in the living room. It will take about 6 to 8 weeks from planting the bulb to flowering. After flowering, cut the flower off so that it cannot set seed, because this takes energy and depletes the bulb. Keep watering until the foliage turns yellow and then put the plant away in the cool. Remove the bulb from the pot in September, clean it, and repot it in fresh compost.

Hyacinthus (hyacinth)

ORIGIN: eastern Mediterranean

The cultivars of *Hyacinthus orientalis* are among the best-known of the bulbs, with dense spikes of beautifully-perfumed flowers, which can be white, pink, salmon, red, light blue and deep purple. Special treatment has created *H. multiflorus*, with multiple stems and smaller flower heads.

Hyacinthus *'Blue Jacket' with* Iris danfordiae   *Previous pages:* Narcissus 'W.P. Milner'

After the first year, hyacinths produce much looser flowers

CARE

Bulbs planted at the beginning of September will be in flower for Christmas. Pot them up with their noses just peeping above the compost and then put them in a cool, dark place. Water regu-

larly. Once the flower buds are clearly visible, move them to a warmer position. When you can see some colour showing, you can bring them into the living room. The cooler you can keep them, the longer they will last. After flowering, plant them out in a sunny spot in the garden. To grow hyacinths in vases, see 'Growing in water' earlier in this chapter.

Narcissus

ORIGIN: Southwest and Southern Europe
To many people narcissi-daffodils-mean spring, and in the depths of winter we look forward eagerly to seeing the cheerful yellow, white, yellow and orange, or white and orange flowers. There are several cultivars that can be successfully grown indoors. The best large-flowered cultivars are the yellow 'Dutch Master', 'Carlton' and 'Golden Harvest', the white and orange

Narcissus

Narcissus 'February Gold'

'Flower Record' and the yellow and orange 'Fortune'. Good small-flowered cultivars include the yellow 'February Gold', 'Peeping Tom' and 'Tête à Tête'. But perhaps the best known of all is the fragrant 'Paperwhite'.

CARE

I described the method of growing 'Paperwhite' earlier in this chapter under the heading 'Growing in water'. After planting, narcissi need a period of cold, during which they must be kept dark. This could be in a garage or shed, or they can be plunged into the soil in the garden. 'Paperwhite' and the yellow 'Soleil d'Or' are the only varieties that can go straight into the light. Water them occasionally. When the shoots are

Left: Narcissus *'Paperwhite'*

Right: Narcissus *'Tête à Tête'*

Below: Narcissus *'Tête à Tête'*

showing well above the surface, you can move them to a lighter position and, once the flower buds start to show, they can go into the living room. Yet again, the cooler they are, the longer they will last for you to enjoy. After flowering, you can plant the bulbs out in the garden-with the exception of 'Paperwhite'.

Oxalis (wood sorrel, lucky clover)

ORIGIN: Mexico and South America

Although several varieties of oxalis are sold as house plants, they can find conditions in the average living room too warm. Put them in a cooler room, or find a spot for them in the garden during the summer.

Oxalis grows from rhizomes. The leaf of *Oxalis deppei*-lucky clover-is made up of four bright green leaflets. The small pink flowers with their yellow centres are borne in small clusters on slender stems.

Oxalis deppei

The cultivar 'Alba' has white flowers, and 'Iron Cross' has brown markings on the leaflets that resemble a rust-brown cross.

O. regnellii has plain green, long-stemmed, three-lobed leaves and white flowers. *O. triangularis*-a variety developed in 1988-has a fairly large, three-lobed leaf in a striking brownish purple with a darker V-shaped marking. The leaves and the pink flowers close at night and sometimes when the weather is dull. The cultivar 'Mijke' has an aubergine-coloured leaf without any marking.

Below: Oxalis triangularis

Right: lucky clover (Oxalis deppei)

Veltheimia

O. rubra (syn. O. floribunda) also has a dark bronze leaf and pale to deep pink flowers. The cultivar 'Alba' has white flowers. The yellow-flowering annual weed, yellow sorrel *(O. corniculata),* is sometimes sold in hanging pots.

CARE

None of the oxalis grown in pots as house plants will thrive in a warm room. Keep the compost moist at all times while they are in growth and feed with a liquid house plant fertilizer every two weeks.

When the foliage starts to turn yellow, give the plant less water until it has completely wilted. Stop watering altogether now, and leave the plant to overwinter at 5°C (40°F). In spring, clean the rhizomes and pot them up in fresh potting compost at a depth of about 3 cm (1^1/$_2$ inches).

Start watering again-a little at first, increasing the amount and adding fertilizer as new growth appears.

Sinningia (gloxinia)

ORIGIN: Brazil

A tuberous plant with a number of hybrids developed from crosses with the species *Sinningia speciosa.* This is an old-fashioned plant with large, velvety leaves and big, bell-shaped flowers growing from the centre. They can be white, pink, blue or purple, single or semi-double.

The plant is generally known as the gloxinia, but this name actually belongs to a member of the *Sinningia* family.

In addition to the many cultivars of *S. speciosa,* *S. cardinalis* is another attractive house plant. As the name indicates, it has bright red flowers. They are very different from the gloxinias: the flowers are tubular and are borne horizontally in clusters on upright spikes.

This plant is also sometimes sold as *Gesneria* or *Rechsteineria.*

CARE

These plants will not tolerate sun, but they do need plenty of light: a window facing east or north is ideal.

While they are growing and flowering they like a moist, but not wet compost. Since the leaves often cover the edge of the pot, it is easier to water the plant from the bottom. This also helps to increase humidity, which is absolutely crucial.

Gloxinias hate getting water on the leaves, so do not mist or spray. Always use tepid softened water and feed regularly with house plant fertilizer. Reduce the water and stop feeding after flowering.

Let the plant die right back and then keep the tuber dry in the pot in a cool place. Repot in fresh compost in the spring, potting it up with the top of the tuber just below the surface. Start it growing again by gradually increasing the amount of water and moving it to a warmer place.

Previous pages: Sinningia cardinalis

Below: Sinningia speciosa

Tulipa (tulip)

ORIGIN: Southeast Europe and Asia Minor

For early blooms your best choices are the red 'Brilliant Star' and 'Merry Christmas', the yellow 'Joffre', the red and yellow 'Plaisir' and the red and cream 'Pinocchio'. These can be followed a little later by a great many other varieties, including the double yellow 'Monte Carlo', the double red 'Stockholm', the single red 'Paul Richter' and 'Topscore', the ever-popular red and white 'Merry Widow' (also sold as 'Lustige Witwe') and the pink 'Rosario' and 'Prelude'. New hybrids are being developed all the time.

CARE

Once you have potted up the bulbs, put the pots in a dark, cool place (about 9°C, 48°F). When the shoots are about 5 cm (2 inches) long, move them to a lighter position, but continue to keep them cool. Do not bring the pots into the warm until the flower buds begin to show colour.

Veltheimia (forest lily)

ORIGIN: South Africa

An old-fashioned bulb with long, green, wavy-edged leaves. The sturdy stem bears a spike of tubular, deep pink flowers reminiscent of the red-hot poker *(Kniphofia)*.

CARE

Unlike most bulbs, *Veltheimia capensis* has a dormant period in the summer and does not come into flower until early spring. Pot up the large bulb in late autumn, using potting compost to which you have added some loam. Plant the bulb so that two-thirds is showing above the surface of the compost and simply leave the pot in a light place.

Start watering as soon as you see the first signs of growth. While the foliage is growing, the plant will be quite happy in the living room, but after this it needs a temperature of no more than 12°C (55°F). The forest lily also likes to be kept cool while it is in flower. Keep the compost slightly moist and feed with a liquid house plant fertilizer every two weeks. Let the compost dry out completely in the summer and do not feed. Put the pot outside during this period. Repot the bulb in autumn.

CHAPTER 6

Orchids and bromeliads

People have always been fascinated by orchids-probably because they look so exotic. When we talk about orchids, we usually mean the species that grow in the tropics and need very high humidity to thrive. Now hybridization has created orchids that can cope with a less sultry climate and rather lower humidity. In this chapter we shall be looking only at the toughest varieties-plants that can be grown in the house, and at the bromeliads.

Cattleya

Orchids

Although there are still native orchid species growing wild in Britain, they are not the type that we could grow indoors-even if they were not protected by law. The orchids growing wild in Europe are terrestrial, which means that they simply grow in the soil, where they can only live in symbiosis with particular fungi.

In their native surroundings, the exotic orchids we so admire and are familiar with as house plants or cut flowers usually grow in trees. Leaves collect in the forks of trees, rot down into humus and provide the perfect home for orchids. The high humidity in the rainforest encourages magnificent growth.

If you want to grow these spectacular plants at home, you will have to ensure that the humidity is kept up. This can often be difficult. One way of ensuring that the air is humid enough is to put the plant in a cache pot and stand this in turn in a shallow container of water. Another method is to place the orchid in its pot on an upturned saucer and stand this in a container of water. If you find this unattractive, you can fill the tray with pebbles or marbles to conceal the saucer. It is also helpful to mist the leaves and stems every day, using soft water at room temperature.

Since the plants are not particularly attractive when they are not in flower, it is best not to bring your orchids into the living room until they are in bud.

Aside from the microclimate, orchids also have other requirements. They will not tolerate fertilizer in the concentrations you would normally give your other house plants. You will probably need to dilute it by as much as ten times, so it is well worth while investing in a special orchid

Orchids for sale in Amsterdam's flower market

A magnificent display of orchids

fertilizer. If you want to repot an orchid you would be advised to use a compost specially formulated for orchids.

Orchid compost is light and contains tree bark, fern roots and sphagnum moss. You will also see orchids fixed to a piece of bark. These species need really high humidity and you would have to have a special growing case for them. The compost in a basket dries out fairly quickly and is less suitable for the living room. Orchids must never be allowed to stand in waterlogged compost or the roots will rot.

Cattleya

ORIGIN: Central and South America
An epiphytic orchid with thick rhizomes and pseudobulbs, bearing one or two fairly large, leathery leaves.

The flowers of the single-leaved varieties are quite large; the two-leaved types have far more flowers, but they are smaller. The most popular form is *Cattleya* x *laeliocattleya*, which has large purple flowers.

CARE

This orchid likes plenty of light but very little sun, except in winter. Most epiphytic orchids (the ones that grow in trees) have pseudobulbs and need a rest period after flowering. At this time they should be given no fertilizer and very little water, although the pseudobulbs must not be allowed to dry out. In spring they need a lot of soft water at room temperature and orchid fertilizer once every two weeks. Once the pseudobulbs are fully developed reduce the water to encourage the plant to flower, otherwise it will simply keep on producing more leaves. Repot the plant into a mixture of sphagnum moss and fern roots every four to five years. Good drainage is essential. Make sure that the humidity is always high.

Cymbidium

ORIGIN: Southeast Asia, Australia and New Zealand
In recent years this orchid has become increasingly popular as a flowering house plant. It is one of the easiest orchids to grow indoors. The

Cattleya

long, grass-like leaf of this plant is dull and not particularly attractive. The foliage and the long flower stems grow from large pseudobulbs. The beautifully marked, waxy flowers occur in a great many delicate pastel shades. The miniature varieties are smaller in all respects and ideal for growing indoors.

CARE

Like many other orchids the *Cymbidium hybrids* like high humidity and are consequently best grown in a greenhouse. However, if you take the plant's likes and dislikes into account there is no reason why you should not succeed with them indoors.

Put the plant in a bright position, out of direct sunlight. The night-time temperature should drop to 17°C (63°F) in summer, and a few degrees lower in winter.

Stand the plant in its cache pot in a container of water to keep the humidity as high as possible.

Mist daily with soft water, particularly if the central heating is on.

Water slightly less in winter, but take care not to let the roots get too dry.

You can check this by looking at the pseudobulbs, which start to shrivel if they dry out. You should feed the plant every two weeks while it is in flower.

Ludisia (syn. Haemaria)

ORIGIN: Asia

At first glance *Ludisia discolor*, with its attractively marked foliage, does not look like an orchid, but if you look very closely at the tiny individual florets, you will see that they are indeed orchid-like.

This terrestrial orchid has creeping rhizomes and dark, chestnut brown leaves with fine veining in red or gold. The fragrant flowers are white with a yellow lip.

Cattleya 'Cinnabar'　　　　　　　Right: Cymbidium

Cymbidium

Cymbidium eburneum

CARE

This is a plant for a north-facing window or, better still, a shady spot in a warm, humid greenhouse. If you grow it indoors you will have to create these conditions as far as possible. Keep the compost reasonably moist. Water from below using tepid water. Feed with special orchid fertilizer once a month.

Miltonia (pansy orchid)

ORIGIN: Central and South America

Most miltonias come from the Andes, where they grow high in the tree canopy, close to the light. Old prints from the nineteenth century, when the plant was very much in fashion, often show this pansy-like orchid.

Hybridization has produced plants suitable for indoor cultivation. The plant has obvious pseudobulbs that serve as moisture reservoirs. The flowers are just like enormous pansies. They are beautifully marked and come in a great many colours and shades.

CARE

Miltonia likes to be fairly cool: around 20-24°C (68-75°F) during the day and 12-15°C (55-60°F) at night. This orchid likes plenty of light but not too much sun.

A window facing east, west or north would be fine. Water with soft water at room temperature and feed with orchid fertilizer once a month. The air humidity must be kept high so mist the plant every day. Avoid spraying the flower, since this causes unsightly spotting.

Oncidium (butterfly orchid)

ORIGIN: South America

There are around 350 species of oncidiums, most of which are epiphytic.

A great deal of hybridization has resulted in cultivars that can be grown indoors. They have fairly small flowers, usually with very attractive markings. The flowers are borne on long stems which sway at the slightest breath of air. The best known forms are the maroon-speckled yellow 'Susie Kaufman' and the red and white 'Cherry Baby'.

CARE

This orchid can take bright light but it will not tolerate full sun. Water the plant sparingly, but do not let it dry out. Plunge it regularly in a bowl of soft, tepid water to which you should add orchid fertilizer once a month. After flowering, put the plant in a cool place (about 15°C, 60°F) and give it very little water, but do not allow the pseudobulbs to dry out. Make sure the plant has fresh air and high humidity.

Right: Ludisia discolor

Below: the beautifully marked leaf of Ludisia

Left: Miltonia

Above: Miltonia

Below: Oncidium

Below: Oncidium

Oncidium

Paphiopedilum

Paphiopedilum (ladies' slipper)

ORIGIN: Asia, the Moluccas and New Guinea
The ladies' slipper and *Cymbidium* are the best-known orchids for growing as house plants. The name of the genus derives from 'Paphia', another name for Venus, and the Greek word 'pedilon', which means shoe. There are a great many species and cultivars in a range of colours-many of them multicoloured and beautifully marked.
CARE
This terrestrial orchid likes light, but not direct sun. The ideal temperature is 16-21°C (60-70°F) during the day and 13-16°C (55-60°F) at night. The species with spotted leaves like to be a little warmer. An ideal night temperature is about 17°C (63°F); the daytime temperature should be 21-27°C (70-80°F). Water every three to five days. After flowering, cut back on the water for

about four weeks, making sure that the plant is not too wet. The humidity must be kept high, particularly in the spring and summer. Repot the plant once every three to four years in a mixture of equal parts sphagnum moss and fern root. You can also add some peat and bark. Put a layer of crocks or clay pebbles at the bottom of the pot.

Phalaenopsis (moth orchid)

ORIGIN: India to Northern Australia and the Philippines
The plant's name is a contraction of the Greek words 'phalaina' (moth) and 'opsis' (like). It is an epiphytic orchid that grows in trees on the fringes of the forest. Phalaenopsis is one of the easiest orchids to grow as a house plant and also makes an excellent cut flower. The white cultivar is often used in bridal bouquets. The food re-

serve is stored not in pseudobulbs but in the thick stems and broad, fleshy leaves. If well cared for, the plant will flower for at least nine months at a time. The flower stem, on which new buds constantly appear, becomes longer and longer, and starts to branch. The old flowers shrivel and drop off, but they are often still so attractive that they can be used as dried flowers.

CARE

You need to be on your guard if you buy a plant while it is in flower. If the weather is cold (below 15°C, 60°F), you would be wise to buy your plant from a heated shop and make sure it is very well packed. When you get it home, put it in a warm, light spot, out of the sun and, above all, away from any vegetables or fruit. Vegetables and fruit give off gases that can have a harmful effect on many flowering plants-and this orchid is one of them. This plant hates draughts. Always water it with rainwater or softened water at room temperature. Make sure that the water can drain away freely, since the roots must not become waterlogged. You can also plunge the pot in water every now and then, making sure that it drains thoroughly afterwards. Never leave any water standing on the

Phalaenopsis *'Christmas Tree'*

Following pages: Phalaenopsis *'Temple Cloud'*

crown of the plant. This orchid also likes the highest humidity you can give it. After flowering, let the plant rest at temperature of at least 12°C (55°F). Reduce the water and do not feed. The plant wants a lot of light during this period, and even some sun. Only repot when absolutely necessary since the roots are easily damaged. Put in a good drainage layer of crocks or clay pebbles and use special orchid compost.

x *Vuylstekeara*

ORIGIN: the result of crosses between *Cochloidea, Miltonia* and *Odontoglossum*
The best known cross is 'Plush' a plant which bears velvety red flowers with a yellow spot in the centre. The large lip has striking white markings. The flowers are carried on long stems.

x Vuylstekeara cambria 'Plush'

Aechmea fasciata

CARE
This plant likes to be in a bright position and will not tolerate direct sunlight. Put a generous layer of drainage material into the pot and top up with a light compost. Use softened water at room temperature and keep the humidity high. If you can create these conditions, you can grow this plant in your living room. In the winter it needs to be kept cooler (about 10°C, 50°F). Water less at this time and do not feed the plant.

Bromeliads

Bromeliads are a very special group of plants with long, tough, often serrated leaves growing from the centre. These leaves catch rainwater and lead to the tubular centre that serves as a water reservoir. In large specimens in the wild this 'urn' can hold up to 50 litres (11 gallons) of water.
The 'flower', primarily coloured bracts with usually insignificant true flowers, also grows from the centre. As a rule, you will buy a plant in

flower, but this is already coming to the end of its days. After flowering, the rosette of leaves will die back. Fortunately, offsets will have formed around the parent plant and these can be grown on.

This process requires considerable skill and you will only succeed if you have green fingers and a heated greenhouse, where you can create high humidity. However, you can take comfort from the fact that a flowering plant will still give you months of pleasure.

Bromeliaceae originate in the tropical rainforests of South America, where they grow on tree stumps and in the forks of branches, where dead leaves and moisture accumulate to form a fertile bed for these plants. Spray bromeliads and always water them with softened (boiled) water or rainwater. Always keep the compost moderately moist. All bromeliads like high air humidity and partial to total shade. The temperature in the room must not be allowed to drop below 18°C (65°F).

Aechmea (urn plant)

The best-known and most widely grown bromeliad is *Aechmea fasciata*, a fairly large plant with broad, grey-speckled and banded strap-like leaves. The pink flowers, which shade to purple later, are concealed among the pink, pointed and sharply serrated bracts, which form a conical flower head. 'Morgana' is the best-known cultivar.

Guzmania minor *hybrid*

Neoregelia *'Flandria'*

Guzmania (scarlet star)

The leaf of this bromeliad is predominantly plain green. The coloured bracts are usually red, although they can be orange or yellow. The flower head is knot-shaped or forms a long, straggly spike. *Guzmania* 'Wittmackii' has a lax growth habit and pale purple bracts.

CARE

Fill the 'urn' in the centre occasionally, using softened water.

Neoregelia (blushing bromeliad)

Like *Aechmea*, *Neoregelia* forms a round plant. The leaf is green *(N. carolinae)* or variegated

with long cream or yellow stripes: *N.* 'Flandria', with a coloured border only, and *N.* 'Tricolor Perfecta' with several stripes along the main vein.

The flowers are in the centre of the rosette. The leaves surrounding the centre 'blush' as they get closer to it-usually red, but pink to lilac in *N. concentrica*.

Tillandsia

Most of the 400 different tillandsias have rather poor flowers. Some are terrestrial, others epiphytic. The species grown most frequently as a flowering plant is *T. cynea*. This is a plant with tough, slender green leaves from the centre of which emerges a flat comb with pink bracts and tiny mauve flowers.

Vriesea

The leaf of *Vriesea* is usually green, sometimes banded in a lighter colour. Many of them bear flat, sword-shaped flower heads in which the bracts provide the showy effect. There are also cultivars with multiple flower heads. These are usually red, and occasionally yellow.

CARE

Like other bromeliads, *Vriesea* will also appreciate being given water in the 'urn' from time to time.

Right: Vriesea psittacina

Vriesea x poelmannii *'White Line'*

Vriesea *flower (detail)*

Photography credits

The photographs in this book were taken by the individuals and organizations below. The page number and place on the page are as follows [key: b. = below, r. = right, l. = left, c. = centre, a. = above]

Nico Vermeulen: 10/11; 12 a.r.; 13 b.; 14; 15 b.; 16; 17; 18 a.l., b.r.; 19 b.; 20/21; 22; 25; 26 a.r.; 27; 28/29; 30; 31; 33; 34; 35 b.r.; 36; 37; 39 b.l.; 40; 41; 42; 44; 45; 46; 48 a.l.; 49; 50/51; 52 a.l., a.r., b.r.; 53 a.r.; 54/55; 56; 57; 58; 59; 60/61; 62; 63; 64 a.r., b.l., b.r.; 65; 68; 70; 71 a.l.; 72; 73; 76; 77; 78; 79 b.r.; 81; 82/83; 84; 85; 86.

Index